Not by Bread Alone

Daily Reflections for Lent 2014

Bishop Robert F. Morneau

LITURGICAL PRESS
Collegeville, Minnesota

www.litpress.org

Cover design by Ann Blattner. Photo: Thinkstock by Getty.

ISSN: 1550-803X

ISBN: 978-0-8146-3475-2   978-0-8146-3477-6 (ebook)

Introduction

Two prolific and excellent writers—Frederick Buechner (b. 1926) and Loren Eiseley (1907–77)—have left markings of their human journey. In 1982 Buechner published *The Sacred Journey* and in 1957 Eiseley published *The Immense Journey*. Both works give us insight into two very different pilgrims, one interpreting life in terms of the workings of grace (*sacred*) and the other in terms of a vast (*immense*) trek through a universe that raises startling and complex questions.

Lent is a journey, at once "sacred" and "immense." During these forty days we are invited to cooperate with God's graces and to confront, not shy away from, the big questions of meaning and commitment. The key principle to hang onto is that God is with us every step of the way, beginning with Ash Wednesday and culminating in the agony and joy of Holy Week. How sacred and immense (and intense) is this pilgrimage.

Perhaps the most significant factor in our personal life is companionship. Who are the individuals who travel with us, either because we have chosen them or they have chosen us? For many it will be parents (and, yes, grandparents) and siblings, for others teachers and schoolmates, still others coworkers and neighbors. During Lent we are invited to journey with the people we hear about in the Scriptures: Jesus and the apostles, the scribes and the Pharisees, tax collectors and sinners, those healed and those seeking peace. These companions have much to teach us about our faith and about life. They too have experienced the sacred and immense journey of life.

In *The Great Divorce*, C. S. Lewis writes, "Every one of us lives only to journey further and further into the mountains." Saint John of the Cross also used the image of a mountain to speak of our journey of faith. We seek union with God and we must be willing to climb the narrow, steep way into God's loving presence. That journey involves time for prayer, time for serving the needs of others, time for sacrifice and mortification. Always we come back to Ash Wednesday's injunction: "Pray! Fast! Give alms!"

The journey is indeed sacred and immense, filled with incredible joy and deep sorrow, overflowing with graces and trials, offering the possibility of love and peace. The advice of not traveling alone is paramount. So, during Lent, we band together as we traverse the valleys of life toward God's mountains, knowing that God guides our every step.

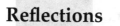

Reflections

The Acceptable Time

Readings: Joel 2:12-18; 2 Cor 5:20–6:2; Matt 6:1-6, 16-18

Scripture:
For I acknowledge my offense,
    and my sin is before me always;
"Against you only have I sinned,
    and done what is evil in your sight." (Ps 51:5-6ab)

Reflection: The pastoral associate conducted a prayer service at the nursing home on Ash Wednesday. She took the blessed ashes from the early morning parish Mass and, after a Scripture reading and a prayer, began to make the sign of the cross on the foreheads of the residents who were unable to get to church. As she approached Mary, who was suffering from dementia, the pastoral associate said, "Mary, turn away from sin . . ." Suddenly, Mary shouted out, "I DON'T HAVE ANY SINS!"

There is a sad humor in this story. Dementia is a terrible illness that puts its victims in a world of unreality. Poor Mary, like the rest of us, cannot claim to be sinless, as much as we would try. We all need conversion for God's grace to touch the unredeemed areas of our minds and hearts, the unredeemed areas of our societies and nations. Lent is a special time to acknowledge our offenses and face the mystery of our sinfulness.

The prophet Joel, with urgency, proclaims the need for repentance. He reminds us that our God is "gracious and merciful . . . slow to anger, rich in kindness." We need not fear. But this turning from sin to God's love and grace involves suffering, for we are about rending our hearts, not our garments. Repentance is costly as is all grace.

Saint Paul, with the same urgency as Joel, reiterates twice that "now" is the acceptable time, now is the day of salvation. This "nowness" precludes procrastination. From the very first day of Lent we cannot delay responding to the call to reconciliation. Paul was one who acknowledged his own sinfulness, so he is speaking from experience.

And how are we to respond? Four words summarize the gospel imperatives: Pray! Fast! Give alms! Do this and we shall live; live in the presence of our loving, forgiving God.

Meditation: Why is it so difficult to acknowledge our sin? Is there a difference between a sense of sinfulness and an individual sin? Why is procrastination so dangerous to spiritual growth?

Prayer: Gracious and merciful God, we need not fear to acknowledge our sin, for you are slow to anger and so rich in kindness. Help us to realize that your mercy always trumps our sins. Help us to turn quickly to the light of your forgiveness and become, like St. Paul, your ambassadors.

Of Great Importance: Obedience

Readings: Deut 30:15-20; Luke 9:22-25

Scripture:
"Today I have set before you
life and prosperity, death and doom.
If you obey the commandments of the LORD . . .
you will live. (Deut 30:15-16)

Reflection: Alan Paton (1903–88), South African writer and political reformer, held the belief that if he stopped being obedient, he would miss something: "I was going to miss something of the greatest importance if I did not treat my life as not being altogether my own property" (*Towards the Mountain*).

Moses knew the same thing. Life was a gift and a responsibility. Everyone has the option of making choices, either to embrace life or to shun it, to live life to the full or attempt to avoid the responsibilities of one's duties. Obedience, that listening and responding to God's will, is of the greatest importance.

Jesus was the obedient one. He embraced his humanity to the full. Suffering and rejection as well as the mystery of death would be part of the deal. Like Moses who taught his people about the meaning of life, Jesus instructed his disciples about the need to carry one's daily cross and to realize that it is in self-giving love, even unto death, that we fulfill our destiny. Doing the Father's will was at the center of the Lord's Prayer. Pope John XXIII chose as his episcopal motto *Obedientia et Pax*—the path to peace lay through obedience. We have here the same paradox as in the gospel: If you save your life, you lose it; if you lose your life, you save it. Such is the nature of our complex life. Peace comes from doing the right thing, not doing what we want. Peace is the great gift that Jesus gave his disciples in the resurrection accounts. Peace, that thing of greatest importance, is offered to us and will be received if we are obedient.

Meditation: What weight do you give to obedience? Is our American approach to freedom compatible with gospel obedience? What is the connection between peace and obedience?

Prayer: Lord Jesus, you were obedient unto death, a death marked by crucifixion. Help us to understand the meaning of obedience; help us to follow in your way, in the spirit of poverty that is our beatitude. May we not miss what is really important in life.

Stubborn Knees; Steely Heart

Readings: Isa 58:1-9a; Matt 9:14-15

Scripture:
For you are not pleased with sacrifices;
   should I offer a burnt offering, you would not accept it.
My sacrifice, O God, is a contrite spirit;
   a heart contrite and humbled, O God, you will not
      spurn. (Ps 51:18-19)

Reflection: Though William Shakespeare would shun the title of spiritual director, many passages in his plays deserve our "spiritual" attention. Here is one example from *Hamlet*: "Bow, stubborn knees; and heart with strings of steel / Be soft as sinews of the new-born babe."

During this season of Lent we do well to evaluate our docility to God's word. After all, a major goal of the spiritual life is to be docile and obedient to the inspirations of the Holy Spirit. This will mean bending our knees in submission to the lordship of Jesus (being a disciple) and having a contrite and humble heart. A spiritual exercise that promotes submission and contrition is asceticism, the self-discipline that opens us up to the stirrings of God's grace.

But there is a difficulty here. God's ways are not our ways, nor are God's thoughts like ours. God is asking us to bend our knees, free the oppressed, and shelter the homeless. God is asking us to have compassionate hearts that break the yoke of enslavement and protect the naked. It is this type of fasting and discipline that God is asking of us. Stubborn knees and steely hearts God spurns; a heart contrite and humble and knees that bend to God's besieging love are truly pleasing to the Lord.

Shakespeare is at it again, speaking of the human heart and therefore of spirituality. In *King Lear*, the king has been rejected and despised by his daughter Regan. Lear cries out, "Then let them anatomize Regan. See what breeds about her heart. / Is there any cause in nature that makes these hard hearts?" God tests the quality of our hearts and is pleased with those that are filled with compassion and humility.

Meditation: Why are the qualities of willfulness and stubbornness so injurious to spiritual growth? What is your understanding of asceticism? Has it more to do with compassion than a rigorous process of self-discipline?

Prayer: Merciful God, may every knee bend before thee and may every heart be open to your presence. Guide us in the way of humility and compassion; transform our attitudes so that we might put on the mind and heart of Christ. Send your Spirit into our lives so that all stubbornness might be vanquished and every string of steel around our hearts might be broken.

I Do!

Readings: Isa 58:9b-14; Luke 5:27-32

Scripture:
Jesus said to them [Pharisees and scribes] in reply,
   "Those who are healthy do not need a physician, but the
      sick do.
I have not come to call the righteous to repentance but
   sinners." (Luke 5:31-32)

Reflection: ". . . in good times and in bad, in sickness and in health." These words uttered at a wedding establish a lifelong covenant. It is a promise of fidelity; it is a commitment at once so profound and so risky.

Long before this formula was written or spoken, God made a similar covenant with us. God said, "I will be true to you in good times and in bad, in sickness and in health." That promise and commitment became manifest in Jesus. Levi and Saul and Mary Magdalene experienced God's coming into their sickness. Jesus restored them to health and reestablished their oneness with the Father (redemption/righteousness). It is in these visitations that we see why Jesus came—for health, for fullness of life, for salvation.

Health is a fragile gift. Within seconds it can disappear—a stroke, a heart attack, an aneurysm. But the health that Jesus came to bring centered just as much on our psychological and spiritual well-being as on our somatic wholeness. Peter was made righteous when he was forgiven for his denials; Zacchaeus was made righteous when he came down from the sycamore tree and allowed Jesus into his heart; the woman with the many demons was made righteous when Jesus freed her from her prison.

One of the deepest hungers of the human heart is for wholeness and integration. All of us need healing because all of us are to some degree ill in mind, heart, and body. Humpty Dumpty, in his great fall, is a symbol of humanity. And Jesus came to put us all back together again, both as individuals and as a community. Lent presents yet another opportunity to revisit God's abiding promise: "I do!"

Meditation: In what ways have you experienced healing? In what ways have you been an agent of healing?

Prayer: Jesus, may we sit at table with you and Levi and experience your healing gaze. May we hear again and again your promise of healing. We are a broken people; we deal with so much dysfunction. Send your spirit of righteousness into our world, into our hearts.

"Moral Counterfeiting"

Readings: Gen 2:7-9; 3:1-7; Rom 5:12-19; Matt 4:1-11

Scripture:
At that time Jesus was led by the Spirit into the desert
    to be tempted by the devil.
He fasted for forty days and forty nights,
    and afterwards he was hungry. (Matt 4:1-2)

Reflection: Adam and Eve were tempted by the serpent; St. Paul was tempted to exasperation over the conduct of certain faith communities; Jesus was tempted by earthly consolations rather than do the Father's will. A significant component of our human condition is this inclination to wrongdoing, to turn away from the hard demands of Christian life and to embrace a life of pleasure and domination.

In a passage from *The Need and the Blessing of Prayer*, the brilliant theologian Karl Rahner writes about our human struggle: "his [man's] hunger for good fortune, his sadness and the melancholy of life that lusts for an anesthetic, his trust in the concrete, his mistrust of the future hereafter, his amazing and uncanny facility for moral counterfeiting which can make good evil and evil good." Human ingenuity is truly amazing. Our ability to "rationalize," to make evil good and good evil, is both uncanny and scary.

Lent is a season to face the temptations that attack us individually and that are embedded in our society. Essentially, these temptations are rooted in the seven deadly sins: pride, anger, lust, gluttony, envy, sloth, greed. We are tempted, be it in the desert or the garden or the mall, to make ourselves the center of the universe, thereby failing in humility. We lose patience so easily. We find it difficult to see sexuality in its true dignity. We overeat and wonder why we are lazy. We are jealous of others. We lose the ability to say "enough." Temptations abound. We need the grace of discernment and courage not to yield to "moral counterfeiting."

Rather than the above translation—"and afterwards he was hungry"—another translation describes Jesus, after his long fast, as being "famished." This word captures well the element of vulnerability regarding temptation. It is when we are famished or weary or ill or stressed out that we are especially susceptible to falling into sin. Thus, we must be on guard since that roaring lion, the devil, attacks us at our weakest points and most vulnerable moments.

Meditation: What is the pattern of temptations in your life? When are your vulnerable moments?

Prayer: Lord Jesus, be with us as we struggle, like you, to be morally authentic. So easily we counterfeit our lives; so easily we yield to the voice of pleasure and possessions. During this Lenten season, be at our side and fend off the wiles of the devil.

Would Do/Should Do

Readings: Lev 19:1-2, 11-18; Matt 25:31-46

Scripture:
And he will separate them [the nations] one from another,
   as a shepherd separates the sheep from the goats.
   (Matt 25:32)

Reflection: As we begin this first full week of Lent we are already reminded of the end time. One day there will be a judgment, a final judgment, of the nations and each of us individually. And the criterion for separating those who are in a right relationship with God from those who have alienated themselves from God's friendship is what we do to one another. The standard is whether or not we have responded to the well-being of others. One need not be a rocket scientist to comprehend the implications of this truth.

So in this first week we "begin with the end in mind," the old philosophical principle that is to guide our actions. The end is union with God and unity with one another. The means of achieving that end is love, a radical concern and respect for everyone. And the byproducts of that union are peace and joy.

In Shakespeare's *Hamlet* we read, "That we would do, / We should do when we would." This phrase expresses the urgency of acting before it is too late. Procrastination is a universal disease and it can be deadly. Our gospel acclamation stresses the importance of not postponing the good God is asking us to do: "Behold, now is a very acceptable time; / behold, now is the day of salvation" (2 Cor 6:2b). We encounter our living and true God in feeding the hungry, in welcoming the stranger, in clothing the naked.

We do well to ponder another Shakespearean insight: "There is a tide in the affairs of men. / Which, taken at the flood, leads on to fortune; / Omitted, all the voyage of their life / Is bound in shallows and in miseries. / On such a full sea are we now afloat, / And we must take the current when it serves, / Or lose our ventures" (*Julius Caesar*).

Meditation: What sense of urgency do you feel when you see someone in need? What role does "begin with the end in mind" play in your spiritual life?

Prayer: Loving and merciful God, help us to respond to our sisters and brothers in need. Every day you give us new opportunities to help others and to make a positive difference in the world. Send your Spirit of love and compassion into our hearts so that we might truly follow in the way of your Son Jesus.

March 11: Tuesday of the First Week of Lent

The Mystery of Prayer

Readings: Isa 55:10-11; Matt 6:7-15

Scripture:
When the just cry out, the LORD hears them,
    and from all their distress he rescues them.
The LORD is close to the brokenhearted;
    and those who are crushed in spirit he saves.
    (Ps 34:18-19)

Reflection: In teaching the disciples how to pray, Jesus speaks out of the conviction given in Psalm 34: "When the just cry out, the LORD hears them" (v. 18a). What Jesus prayed for was that God's name be held holy, that God's kingdom might come, that God's will be done. The focus of the prayer was not on the "pray-er," but on what would give glory to God. Obviously, this is the prayer of a mature person, one who is not always petitioning God for help or asking for forgiveness for sins or even giving thanks for gifts received. Rather, it is a prayer of adoration and reverence.

But we do have an issue here, the issue of "unanswered prayers." What do we say to a person who prays that a son or daughter be healed and the illness continues or death occurs? What about prayers for good weather or a bountiful crop when a nation faces a drought or famine? Then there is the case of war when both sides invoke God for victory.

Given our shortsightedness (spiritual myopia) and our narcissistic tendencies, we fail to understand the heart of the Our Father prayer: "Thy will be done!" Yet even here we live in mystery because we cannot comprehend the long-range vision of our God.

We need faith to believe that "the LORD hears them [the cry of the just], / and from all their distress he rescues them." We need the faith of the psalmist who goes even further: "The LORD is close to the brokenhearted; / and those who are crushed in spirit he saves" (Ps 34:19). For those of us who have had our hearts broken or our spirits crushed, we know the compassion and mercy of our God. Jesus in Gethsemane and on Calvary tasted from the inside the experience of this prayer.

Meditation: How effective is prayer? Does it work? And when it "doesn't," what is your response?

Prayer: Jesus, teach us how to pray and teach us to understand the mystery of prayer. So often our prayers don't seem to be answered. So often we do not experience your rescuing power. Give us your wisdom to know what to pray for and the courage to go on when we do not experience your presence.

An Evil Generation

Readings: Jon 3:1-10; Luke 11:29-32

Scripture:
While still more people gathered in the crowd, Jesus said
    to them,
    "This generation is an evil generation;
    it seeks a sign, but no sign will be given it,
    except the sign of Jonah." (Luke 11:29)

Reflection: Sociologists have a field day in naming generations. A few examples: Arthurian Generation (1433–60), Transcendental Generation (1792–1821), GI Generation (1901–24),
Millennial Generation (1982–2000), and so many other generations in between.

Jesus was not a sociologist but he too labeled the culture
of his times: "an Evil Generation." Perhaps this labeling has
a more universal dimension. Is not evil present in every generation, be it Arthurian, Transcendental, GI, or Millennial?
Are not we all part of the crowds that Jonah and Jesus were
speaking to when the call to conversion rings out? Indeed,
evil abides in every generation and must be confronted.

There is a startling line in Dostoyevsky's *The Brothers
Karamazov*: "They all declare that they hate evil, but secretly
they all love it." Is there a hidden darkness in human nature
that finds evil and iniquity attractive, even desirable? The

Russian novelist articulates a truth that should send us searching for sackcloth and ashes. The English novelist Charles Williams called evil "the blackness of things." It is the mystery of evil that Jesus and Jonah came to confront.

What about our generation? As we venture further and further into the twenty-first century, we must address those areas in our lives that are in need of conversion. These areas might well involve personal relationships, business ethics, political discourse, economic sharing, or psychological health. Evil, the negative of good, creeps into every area of our life and must be rooted out. That is why God keeps sending people like Jonah to cry out in our streets and malls, "Repent!"

Meditation: What is your assessment of our present generation? What thoughts come to mind as you ponder the mystery of evil?

Prayer: Gracious God, we long to be a good generation, a culture that contributes to the building of your kingdom. Yet evil lurks deep within our hearts and our society. Send your Spirit of truth and courage into our lives so that we might discern what you ask of us and do it.

March 13: Thursday of the First Week of Lent

Important Matters

Readings: Esth C:12, 14-16, 23-25; Matt 7:7-12

Scripture:
Queen Esther, seized with mortal anguish,
    had recourse to the LORD. . . .
"Help me, who am alone and have no help but you,
    for I am taking my life in my hand." (Esth C:12, 14b-15)

Reflection: Loneliness and anguish are common human experiences. Queen Esther turned to the Lord for consolation and support. On the human level, she had no one to help her. On the spiritual level, she had faith in a God who had the power to free her from her anguish.

In the May 2012 issue of *The Atlantic*, the lead article asked the question, "Is Facebook Making Us Lonely?" The point was that while Facebook makes many connections, there is very little real bonding and thus the loneliness. The article went on to describe a study done in 1985 where 10 percent of Americans stated that they had no one with whom to discuss "important matters." By 2004, the study indicated that 25 percent of people had no one to talk to regarding significant concerns.

Jesus was aware of human loneliness. He knew the importance of community, of having people with whom we can share our lives. But he also called people to stay close to his Father through a life of prayer. Like Queen Esther, we are to ask, to seek, and to knock. We are to open our minds and hearts to God's providential care. Just as we bring important matters to those with whom we journey, we are to bring important matters to God as well.

And what are some of those important matters? Surely they would include regrets from the past, worries about the future, concerns about our daily affairs. We might do what Raissa Maritain did: "I enter into the presence of God with all my load of misery and troubles. And he takes me just as I am and makes me to be alone with him" (*Raissa's Journal*). Queen Esther and Raissa Maritain have much to teach us.

Meditation: How do you deal with loneliness and anxiety? What role does prayer play in your spiritual life?

Prayer: Gracious and compassionate God, our journey is long and difficult. When we experience isolation and alienation, come to our aid. Assure us of your mercy and love. Help us to reach out to others in their anguish and fears; help us to be instruments of your compassionate care.

God's Great Kingdom

Readings: Ezek 18:21-28; Matt 5:20-26

Scripture:
Jesus said to his disciples:
"I tell you,
    unless your righteousness surpasses that
    of the scribes and Pharisees,
    you will not enter into the Kingdom of heaven."
        (Matt 5:20)

Reflection: Again and again, Jesus draws us back to ponder "the Kingdom of heaven." His personal prayer, and the one handed on to the disciples and us, included the phrase "thy kingdom come." The question today is what gives us entrance into God's kingdom? What is the righteousness that is demanded of us?

On the feast of Christ the King, the church invites us to ponder the mystery of the kingdom of God. Our tradition informs us that the kingdom is one of peace and justice, love and mercy, truth and joy. To be a kingdom person we are called to be agents of light and not darkness, life and not death, love and not hatred. Through the gift of the Holy Spirit we are empowered to become such people, the people of God.

The prophet Ezekiel speaks to two types of people: the wicked person and the virtuous person. God rejoices in those who turn away from evil; God claims that those who turn away from virtue will surely die. God's kingdom is about doing good and turning away from iniquity. God's kingdom is to foster life and live that life to the full.

But for entering the kingdom it is not something that we merit. In the end, we all need the mercy of God because we are all a mixture of good and evil. At times we have turned away from God and sinned; at other times, we have responded to the prompting of the Holy Spirit and have done virtuous deeds.

The theologian Romano Guardini says it quite simply: "Kingdom of God means a state in which God is king and consequently rules" (*The Lord*).

Meditation: What is your understanding of "righteousness"? In what ways can you foster God's kingdom today?

Prayer: Lord Jesus, our king and brother, give us the vision to see what you see, to hear what you hear. May we be agents of your truth and justice in a broken world. Forgive our iniquity and fill us with your grace so that we live and not die.

The Mystery of Love

Readings: Deut 26:16-19; Matt 5:43-48

Scripture:
"For if you love those who love you, what recompense
   will you have?
Do not the tax collectors do the same?" (Matt 5:46)

Reflection: In the Broadway musical *South Pacific* (1958), one
of the hit tunes was "Some Enchanted Evening." The refrain
of the song asked whether anyone could explain the mystery
of two people falling in love. The lyrics inform us that fools
will attempt to give reasons for this phenomenon but wise
people don't even try.

But Jesus, the wisdom of God, plunges into the mystery
of love and challenges us to love not only those whom we
know and respect but also those we consider enemies, individuals who hate and persecute us. Now, try to explain that
to a victim! But God's ways are not our ways, nor are God's
thoughts similar to ours. God is love and the nature of
love is to be indiscriminate and unlimited. God cannot not
love, but whether that love is received or not is another
question.

Moses, God's ancient spokesman, is of the same mind as
Jesus. If God is to be our God, then we must walk in his ways
and observe his commandments. And the first and greatest

of the commandments is that of love. This is not some romantic emotion. Rather, the love demanded of us is filled with respect and responsibility. We are to see the dignity of others and respond to their needs. Erich Fromm, in his book *The Art of Loving*, says it well: "The loving person responds."

The last stanza of George Herbert's poem "Matins" might be an excellent Lenten mantra: "Teach me thy love to know; / That this new light, which now I see, / May both the work and workman show: / Then by a sunbeam I will climb to thee." Unless God teaches us what love is all about, we will remain in darkness.

Meditation: Why do people love one another? Why do they hate one another? What does Herbert's poem say to you?

Prayer: Lord Jesus, the mystery of love is overwhelming. Teach us what it is and give us the grace to be loving, compassionate, and forgiving people. Send us sunbeams every day so we might climb to you, the source of all light, life, and love.

March 16: Second Sunday of Lent

I Am, I See

Readings: Gen 12:1-4a; 2 Tim 1:8b-10; Matt 17:1-9

Scripture:
Jesus took Peter, James, and John his brother,
    and led them up a high mountain by themselves.
And he was transfigured before them. (Matt 17:1-2a)

Reflection: Was Ralph Waldo Emerson correct when he said, "As I am, so I see"? Peter, James, and John saw something new in Jesus on that mountaintop experience. There was some grace given that enabled them to recognize Jesus as more than just another good person. Their eyes were opened and what they saw, the uniqueness and divinity of Jesus, changed their lives. Their "am" was transformed by the transfiguration.

Seeing, like hearing, is a difficult art. We are so preoccupied with life's distractions that we often fail to notice what is right in front of us. In our noisy world, we don't hear very well, be it the cry of the poor or the glory of God in a robin's song. Failure to see and hear diminishes our personality, our "am."

Abram's hearing and obedience are models for us. When the Lord promised to bless him and make his name known, Abram believed in God's word. He then "went as the LORD directed him." Here is a mantra that leads to holiness—doing what the Lord tells us.

Although St. Paul never encountered Jesus on the mountaintop, he did meet Christ on the road to Damascus. Paul would go on to tell how Christ robbed death of its power and gave life and immortality to all who believed. Abram and Paul knew that it was truly good to hear and follow the Lord's way.

In our better moments, when silence empowers us to hear the Lord's voice, we too might be invited up to the mountaintop, or down by the seashore, or along a solitary road in the country, and there encounter Jesus. Like Peter, we might be tempted to hang onto the experience and build a couple of tents. But those moments of encounter come and go, and then we plunge back into our ordinary, daily routines. It is here that we live the grace received in moments of prayer and meditation. It is here, in compassionate love, that we realize the encounter was truly authentic.

Meditation: Where have you encountered Christ? What is the quality of your seeing and hearing? In what ways has your understanding of Jesus grown over the years?

Prayer: Transfigured Jesus, grace us with insight and wisdom. Open our eyes and ears to the glory of your Father. Help us to experience the divine milieu in which we live. Draw us onto the mountaintop.

God: Great and Awesome

Readings: Dan 9:4b-10; Luke 6:36-38

Scripture:
Lord, great and awesome God,
  you who keep your merciful covenant toward those
    who love you
  and observe your commandments! (Dan 9:4b)

Reflection: In his famous *Confessions*, St. Augustine addresses God: "The idea I had of you was falsehood and not truth, a fiction of my own littleness, not the solid ground of your beatitude." The mystery of God is overwhelming for our finite intelligence, our "littleness." Daniel the prophet used words like great and awesome and merciful to describe his experience of the Deity. And even these words, noble as they are, cannot capture the essence of our triune God.

Like St. Augustine, C. S. Lewis also struggled with his concept of God. With candor, Lewis observes, "My idea of God is not a divine idea. It has to be shattered time after time" (*A Grief Observed*). Probably the "best ideas" of God, those categories that come closest to giving us some insight into the divine mystery, are love and mercy. We hear in the gospel today that God is merciful; we read in the epistles of St. John that God is love. Herein lies the greatness and awesomeness of our God.

This attempt to understand and "name" our God has practical consequences. Made to the image and likeness of God, we are called to be loving and merciful. This love is expressed in active concern for others; this mercy is manifest in forgiving others as God has forgiven us.

During this Lenten season our challenge will be to confront sins opposed to love and mercy. Too often we fail in responding to people in need; too often we hold grudges and refuse to forgive. In this season of conversion, we ask our merciful and loving God, our awesome and great God, to send the Holy Spirit into our hearts and into our fragile, broken world.

Meditation: How has your concept of God changed over the years? What categories help you to appreciate the mystery of God?

Prayer: Triune God, you reveal yourself to us in the person of Jesus. In Christ we see your love and mercy; in Christ we hear words of forgiveness and tender concern. Help us to be good disciples and to keep your law.

White Wool/White Snow

Readings: Isa 1:10, 16-20; Matt 23:1-12

Scripture:
Come now, let us set things right,
    says the LORD:
Though your sins be like scarlet,
    they may become white as snow;
Though they be crimson red,
    they may become white as wool. (Isa 1:18)

Reflection: For Isaiah the prophet, the colors for sin are scarlet and crimson red, whereas his color for grace is white, grace being white as snow and wool. As a prophet, Isaiah is concerned about righteousness, setting things right between God and humanity. Doing evil injures and breaks the covenant relationship; doing good—hearing the orphan's plea and defending the widow and redressing wrongs—sustains and deepens our relationship with God and others.

The prophets and evangelists have a double concern: our relationship with God and our relationship with one another. Although we distinguish between the two, they are intimately related since we are but a single family with God as our common Father. Even in our church architecture we are reminded of our double relationship. "Church architecture, whatever the style, should carry the eye horizontally towards the altar of the Eucharist, and vertically towards God" (Peter Hebblethwaite, *Paul VI: The First Modern Pope*). The horizontal and vertical dimensions of our faith life must be constantly addressed.

Jesus confronted the scribes and Pharisees for failing to integrate the vertical and horizontal dimensions of the covenant. Their leaders laid heavy burdens on the people; they preached but did not practice; they sought out places of honor and prestige. Jesus called them to humility, a grace as white as wool, and he admonished them for their pride, a sin of scarlet.

In the classic novel *The Scarlet Letter*, Nathaniel Hawthorne offers an admonition regarding the scarlet sin of adultery: "Among many morals which press upon us from the poor minister's miserable experience, we put only this into a sentence: 'Be true! Be true! Be true! Show freely to the world, if not your worst, yet some trait whereby the worst may be inferred!'"

Meditation: Are there any relationships in your life that need to be set straight? How do you integrate the horizontal and vertical dimensions of your faith?

Prayer: Gracious and merciful God, our sins are crimson red and we stand in need of your forgiveness. In Jesus you have set things right and have washed us clean. Take away our pride and give us the white grace of humility. Come, Holy Spirit, come.

Attentiveness/Responsiveness

Readings: 2 Sam 7:4-5a, 12-14a, 16; Rom 4:13, 16-18, 22; Matt 1:16, 18-21, 24a

Scripture:
[B]ehold,
> the angel of the Lord appeared to him [Joseph] in a
> dream and said, "Joseph, son of David,
> do not be afraid to take Mary your wife into your
> home." (Matt 1:20b)

Reflection: There are two fundamental elements in our spiritual life: attentiveness and responsiveness. Everyone is called to be alert to the visitations of our God. More, everyone is called to respond to the stirrings and the proddings of the Holy Spirit.

God's intrusions are many and varied. God comes to us through the mystery of creation, through the Sacred Scriptures, through the richness of our sacramental life, in daily experiences and historical events, in the depth of our conscience. God can even come to us through our subconscious life in dreams. This was the experience of Joseph in the Old Testament, of Joseph, the spouse of Mary, in the New Testament.

Intrusions are one thing, the response is another. When the angel departed, Joseph did what the Lord asked and took Mary into his home. Here is the obedience of faith that is part of every disciple: doing what God wills. And so often that doing is done without any clarity about consequences. A radical trust is essential. Both Joseph and Mary had that quality.

The Spanish philosopher José Ortega y Gasset asserted, "Tell me to what you pay attention and I will tell you who you are." Perhaps he wrote elsewhere, "Tell me what you respond to and I will tell you what your destiny is." Attention and response! Our identity and our destiny are wrapped up in these two words.

Meditation: Why is attention deficit disorder a serious issue? Why is being nonresponsive so dangerous? To what or to whom do you give your attention; to what do you respond?

Prayer: Lord God, send your angel into our lives and our history. Grace us with keen attention and empower us to respond unreservedly to what you ask. We ask for the intercession of St. Joseph, as one who heard your call and did your will. We ask for the intercession of Mary, his spouse and our mother.

Our Probing God

Readings: Jer 17:5-10; Luke 16:19-31

Scripture:
I, the LORD, alone probe the mind
    and test the heart,
To reward everyone according to his ways,
    according to the merit of his deeds. (Jer 17:10)

Reflection: Our probing God does a thorough job. God probes the mind; God probes the heart; God probes our conscience. No stone—or, rather, no thought, feeling, or deed—goes unnoticed. Each of us, like the rich man and Lazarus too, has a cognitive, affective, and behavioral domain that will be tested and evaluated.

The cognitive domain! Thoughts matter. The rich man, unconcerned about the poor, was aware of the law (Moses) and the prophets. He was given God's game plan and could not use the excuse of ignorance. But the rich man, from the land of the dead, knew that his brothers too had access to prophetic messages. Like himself, the brothers needed something more to awaken them to their social responsibilities. Maybe, just maybe, if someone from the dead would return, the brothers would come to their senses. "Fat chance," says the Lord.

The affective domain! Let's give credit where credit is due. The rich man was concerned about his brothers. He had some grain of compassion, at least for his own kin, if not for the stranger Lazarus. But that seems to be the limit. God probed the rich man's heart and found it cold, as cold as the unconverted Ebenezer Scrooge. Caught up in his fine cloth and sumptuous food, the rich man ignored Lazarus and his plight.

The behavioral domain! Thought and affectivity have the power to shape our behavior. The rich man did not *do* anything; he just simply remained absorbed in himself and his comfort and ignored the poor. God probes the conscience and the rich man found himself guilty.

The Welsh poet R. S. Thomas wondered if perhaps it was in silence that God was hiding from our search. Long before we search for God, in silence or creation or salvation history, God is already searching for us, probing our minds, hearts, and behavior with his graced-filled light.

Meditation: How do you respond to a "probing" God? Why do thoughts and feelings matter so much? And behavior? What is the quality of your social responsibility?

Prayer: Loving and probing God, be gentle with us. Our minds are so clouded, our hearts so fragile, our behavior so ambiguous. Have mercy on our weakness and send your Spirit to enlighten our minds, enkindle our hearts, and empower us to know and do your will.

Silver: Twenty, Thirty Pieces

Readings: Gen 37:3-4, 12-13a, 17b-28a; Matt 21:33-43, 45-46

Scripture:
They sold Joseph to the Ishmaelites for twenty pieces of
   silver. (Gen 37:28a)

Reflection: Judas cut a deal with the religious authorities
and sold Jesus for thirty pieces of silver (Matt 26:15). Cain
invited his brother Abel for a walk out in the field and killed
him (Gen 4:8). Peter, when questioned about his relationship
with Jesus, denied that he knew him (Matt 26:70).

We all live east of Eden. We are all marred, flawed, imper-
fect human beings. Lent provides an opportunity for self-
examination, but even more, for focusing on a God who is
with us and who shares the Spirit of wisdom and courage.
We need not get caught up in scheming and stoning, in our
plotting and killing, in our denials and betrayals.

Reuben was a good man. He had a plan to save his brother.
Though the plan failed, a larger plan began to unfold. Joseph
would be taken to Egypt and would eventually "save" his
brothers and people from death.

Jesus, besides being our Savior, was a storyteller. The parable about the landowner is a parable about us. We each have
been given a vineyard to tend. One day we must give an
accounting of our stewardship. Hopefully, as tenants, we

will not have to repent of injuries done to others—no beatings, no stonings, no killings. Rather, may we hear those glorious words about being a good steward of God's gifts and a faithful servant.

Reuben! Judah! Joseph! Jesus! Biblical people who, upon closer examination, have something to say about our lives. In God's grace, may those sayings fill us with light, love, and life.

Meditation: Whom do you identify with in today's readings? If Adam and Eve had gone west of Eden instead of east, would we have a different world?

Prayer: Lord Jesus, keep telling us stories. Our journey, immense and long, is filled with much darkness and confusion. Help us to see your providential love in the life of Joseph and Reuben. Help us to tend your garden well.

March 22: Saturday of the Second Week of Lent

Logic and Affectivity: Paths of Knowledge

Readings: Mic 7:14-15, 18-20; Luke 15:1-3, 11-32

Scripture:
"Coming to his senses he [prodigal son] thought,
  'How many of my father's hired workers
  have more than enough food to eat,
  but here am I, dying from hunger.'" (Luke 15:17)

Reflection: Logic is important. Clear thinking draws us near to the truth and opens the gate to freedom. In the gospel parable about the prodigal son, we hear how the son "came to his senses" and figured out an alternative to dying of hunger. The rest of the story is familiar to us.

The elder son, faithful to his duties and loyal to his father, was confronted with a situation that appeared to be poor judgment on the part of his father. The elder son's wayward brother was given the royal treatment despite living a life of dissipation and causing tremendous pain for his father. One would think that the elder son had "come to his senses" and figured out how illogical his father was in treating the prodigal son so mercifully.

But logic is only one way of knowing, of coming to the truth that leads to freedom. Just as valid as reason is our affectivity. The father *felt* deep compassion for the younger son. The father had a tender, forgiving heart. Whatever the motives the prodigal son had for returning, the issue was not the intention but the fact of the return. What was lost was found; what was dead had come back to life.

The prophet Micah speaks of a God who removes guilt and delights in clemency. Our God is prodigal because of his compassion. God casts our sins into the sea and treads our guilt underfoot. We are all the younger son in our seasons of dissipation; we are all the elder son in our times of bitterness.

Meditation: What role do you give to reason and affectivity in coming to know the truth? In what sense is God prodigal?

Prayer: Merciful God, you know our weakness and our stupidity. Help us to come home, to turn from sin and darkness into the grace and light of your love. Fill us with your compassion and draw us into the circle of your peace. May we come to our senses and live forever in your presence.

Evangelization: New and Old

Readings: Exod 17:3-7; Rom 5:1-2, 5-8; John 4:5-42 or 4:5-15, 19b-26, 39a, 40-42

Scripture:
Many of the Samaritans of that town began to believe in
    him [Jesus]
  because of the word of the woman who testified,
  "He told me everything I have done." (John 4:39)

Reflection: Whether we speak of the old or new evangelization, it is all about coming to know and love our God revealed in Jesus. A high school confirmation candidate wrote in her letter requesting the sacrament, "God has been so good to me. I want everyone to know who God is." Is there any better description of evangelization than this?

The anonymous Samaritan woman in today's gospel wanted the townspeople to know who Jesus was. She gave testimony to what happened at Jacob's well: Jesus' respect for her, their personal conversation, her coming to the truth. It was a eucharistic moment that led to profound gratitude and commitment. Truth and freedom were the graces this woman received. She felt compelled to share the Good News.

Saint Paul, one of the greatest evangelists, encountered Christ in an unexpected way, like the Samaritan woman. It wasn't at a well but on a road, a road taking Paul (then Saul) to persecute Christ's followers. We know the rest of the story: Paul came to realize that Christ died for all of us and that God's love was poured out on all creation through the Holy Spirit. Paul felt compelled to spread the story of Jesus, which he did by preaching and writing to Christian communities. His message was clear and concise: we are justified by faith and are now at peace with God through Jesus.

One of the great church documents is the encyclical *Evangelii Nuntiandi* (Evangelization in the Modern World, 1975) by Pope Paul VI. The pope presents a powerful vision of evangelization and various methods for doing that essential mission of the church. Like St. Paul, Pope Paul VI wrote about the Holy Spirit's activity: "It must be said that the Holy Spirit is the principal agent of evangelization: it is he who impels each individual to proclaim the Gospel, and it is he who in the depth of consciences causes the word of salvation to be accepted and understood" (75).

Meditation: What is your understanding of evangelization? In what ways have you shared the good news of God's love for us in Christ through the Holy Spirit?

Prayer: Come, Holy Spirit, come. Empower us to be good evangelists, sharing the good news of salvation in Jesus. May our words and our lives proclaim your love. Deepen our awareness of evangelization as the essential mission of the church.

Good and Courageous Evangelists

Readings: 2 Kgs 5:1-15ab; Luke 4:24-30

Scripture:
Now the Arameans had captured in a raid on the land of Israel
a little girl, who became the servant of Naaman's wife.
(2 Kgs 5:2)

Reflection: In the 1860s, a little girl was kidnapped and sold into slavery in the Sudan. Her name was Josephine Bakhita. Through God's grace, she eventually was taken to Italy, where she joined a religious community. She died in 1947 and was canonized by Pope John Paul II in 2000.

Josephine Bakhita had a religious experience: she knew that she was created, known, loved, and awaited by God. This is essentially the message of the prophets, be the prophet Elisha or Elijah or Isaiah or, *the* prophet, Jesus. The message is fundamentally the same: our providential God created us, abides with us, and gives us the Spirit.

But there is something radically wrong in the city of man. It is not just in refusing to accept a prophet because he is from our hometown. It is something deeper. It has to do with not accepting the message that the prophet comes to deliver. Is it really true that we are known, loved, and awaited by God? Are we truly the object of God's concern and infinite wisdom? Are we, each one, truly an integral part of God's plan, the building of the city of God?

By a special grace, Josephine Bakhita, though severely scarred by her years of captivity, embraced the message of the Gospel. Her faith led her into a life of self-giving and she is now interceding for us in the great cloud of witnesses in heaven.

Meditation: Why is the message of God's love so difficult to appropriate? What message about life do you hand on to your family and friends? Why are prophets killed?

Prayer: Merciful and loving God, grant us the gift of faith. May we come to realize that we are grasped by your love and held tenderly in your heart. May we fulfill our baptismal call to be prophetic, our call to spread the good news of your mercy and love in Jesus. Make us good and courageous evangelists.

Ave Maria

Readings: Isa 7:10-14; 8:10; Heb 10:4-10; Luke 1:26-38

Scripture:
And coming to her [Mary], he [Gabriel] said,
   "Hail, full of grace! The Lord is with you."
But she was greatly troubled at what was said
   and pondered what sort of greeting this might be.
      (Luke 1:28-29)

Reflection: Every Sunday Patrick's sister would come to his apartment and bring him Holy Communion. Patrick, living alone, was blind and suffered from terminal illness. Every Sunday as his sister began the ritual with the Our Father, Patrick would insist on praying the Hail Mary, his favorite and most beloved prayer. A compromise was reached—both prayers were offered.

Ave Maria! "Hail Mary!" Mary, like us, was called by name and her vocation was to welcome Jesus into her life. She did this. She made a radical act of trust even though she did not understand the specifics of God's mysterious plan. Talk about faith! Mary's trusting "fiat" challenges all of us to have confidence in God's will, as strange and mysterious as it might seem.

Gratia plena! "Full of grace!" Mary found favor with God. God's light, love, and life radiated through her being. Yet in all that fullness, Mary lived in the human condition of radical indigence and innate poverty. She had to live with the paradox of fullness and emptiness, of dying and rising, of not knowing and yet "in the know" through simple faith.

Dominus tecum! "The Lord is with you!" God's life is with us in so many ways: through the mystery of creation, in the friendship of family and friends, in our sacramental life and biblical passages, in the movements of our heart. The angel gave Mary, who was deeply troubled, an assurance (a blessed assurance) that God dwelt within her. This indwelling of the Spirit is our innate treasure, the pearl of great price. And Mary was told that she possessed it.

Meditation: What are your favorite prayers? What role does Mary play in your life as a mentor and model, as a teacher and witness of God's ways?

Prayer: Mary, you who are full of grace and yet embrace poverty of spirit, help us to be open to God's plan and to trust as you did. Our journey is often troubled and weary. Our days are often dark and lonely. Send an angel to reassure us of God's presence and maybe, just maybe, we too will become instruments of God's peace and joy.

Your Children's Children

Readings: Deut 4:1, 5-9; Matt 5:17-19

Scripture:
"However, take care and be earnestly on your guard
    not to forget the things which your own eyes have seen,
    nor let them slip from your memory as long as you live,
    but teach them to your children and to your children's
        children." (Deut 4:9)

Reflection: At wedding ceremonies there is a nuptial blessing bestowed upon the newly married couple after the Our Father. One passage from that blessing reads, "Bless them with children and help them to be good parents. May they live to see their children's children."

Parents have many responsibilities: providing for their children's education, monitoring their friendships, encouraging and disciplining, and the list goes on. But there is yet another duty: helping their sons and daughters nurture a faith life. Parents are the first and primary educators in the faith life of their children.

Thus the wise advice of Moses: Take care, be on your guard, and do not forget what God has done for you. God has given us life (our Creator God) and thus parents teach their children to be grateful. Our God has come to heal us and restore us to oneness (our redeeming God manifest in

Jesus). Parents help their children to deal with the mystery of sin and its consequence, alienation. Our God abides with us still (our God as indwelling Spirit). Parents teach their offspring to know that they are temples of the Holy Spirit.

If parenting is done well, there is the possibility that their children will be able to teach their own children about the mystery of God and the meaning of life. But, if care is not taken, if parents are not vigilant, if they forget about the mysteries of faith, future generations will be lost in the cosmos and live in darkness.

Meditation: What are the ways in which you remember what God has done and is doing for you? Were your parents (or you as a parent) vigilant in their duty in helping you grow in your faith life?

Prayer: Gracious God, you continue to create, redeem, and sanctify us. May we be grateful for all that you are doing for us. More, may we help others to come to an understanding of your constant presence and love for us. Make us good parents, good children, good disciples.

Devils and Demons

Readings: Jer 7:23-28; Luke 11:14-23

Scripture:
Jesus was driving out a demon that was mute,
   and when the demon had gone out,
      the mute man spoke and the crowds were amazed.
         (Luke 11:14)

Reflection: Mark Twain (Samuel Langhorne Clemens) was known for his wit, his impressive stage appearance, his ability to hold an audience in the palm of his hand. Mark Twain also wrestled with his demons: extreme loneliness, neurotic guilt and shame, estrangement and isolation. In the complexity of this life, Twain was seeking freedom, a freedom that would rid him of his demons, like the person in today's gospel.

Jesus came to bring us salvation and to set us free from sin and death. Another word for redemption is liberation, the process that rescues us from those divisive attitudes and actions that block our union with God and with one another. Only those who are truly free can be obedient to God's commandments. Liberation leads to faithfulness.

The prophet Jeremiah comments on what might be considered demons: hardness of heart, a stiff neck, the unwillingness to listen to God's voice. As a prophet, Jeremiah sought to help his people pay heed to the voice of God, a voice calling the people to truth and justice. Deafness, not muteness, was the demon afflicting Jeremiah's audience. This deafness rose out of stubbornness and a lack of love.

Demons and devils are not in vogue in our postmodern world. Yet, C. S. Lewis's book *The Screwtape Letters* still speaks to the human condition. Listen to the senior devil Screwtape speaking about God: "He [God] really loves the human vermin and really desires their freedom and continued existence." The devil is trying to plant the germ of unbelief in the heart of every human. By contrast, God's love and God's longing is that we be free and come to the fullness of life. If C. S. Lewis penned the devil's letters, God has penned the Scriptures to remind us of his love and mercy.

Meditation: What demons do you have to wrestle with? Pride? Greed? A hard heart? When have you experienced the grace of freedom?

Prayer: Faithful God, help us to heed your voice and to seek your will. Remove from our minds any untruth and from our hearts any hardness. Without your help we are bound to be enslaved by forces stronger than we are. Send your Spirit of freedom and responsibility into our lives.

God's Kingdom: Near or Far?

Readings: Hos 14:2-10; Mark 12:28-34

Scripture:
And when Jesus saw that he [a scribe] answered with
  understanding,
  he said to him,
  "You are not far from the Kingdom of God."
    (Mark 12:34a)

Reflection: R. S. Thomas (1913–2000), a Welsh poet, wrote a beautiful verse titled "The Kingdom." He begins by stating that the kingdom appears a long way off but then, in a quick turn, says that to get to the kingdom doesn't take any time at all. More, to enter the kingdom doesn't cost anything *if* you have faith and *if* you have compassion.

Jesus was impressed with the scribe's response to his teaching about the two great commandments. Jesus told the scribe directly that he was "not far from the Kingdom of God." The only thing left for the scribe to do was to put his understanding into action, that is, to love God and his neighbor.

Faith is one of the doors into the kingdom. This virtue makes us aware that "God is Lord alone!" (Mark 12:29b). But it is more than awareness; it is also a commitment. We come to realize that we are in a covenant relationship, one rich in mutuality and reciprocity. Just as God is faithful to us, we are called to be faithful to God by being loving and compassionate. In a faith-filled life, God's self-giving is experienced in some way, mysterious to both our minds and hearts. Our task is first and foremost one of hospitality, receiving in gratitude God's loving presence.

A second door into the kingdom of God is compassion or love. This love of God and our neighbor is extremely demanding. In fact, love's synonym is sacrifice, that total self-giving we see in the life of Jesus. Indeed the kingdom is not far from any of us if we have the compassion of Christ and the faith of Mary, his mother.

Meditation: When have you experienced the kingdom as being far away, as being right around the corner? Are there other doors into the kingdom besides faith, compassion, and love?

Prayer: Heavenly Father, may your kingdom come into our hearts and into your world. We find it so difficult to love fully, so demanding to love as Jesus loved. Send your Spirit into our lives that we might emulate Mary and the great saints who believed deeply and who loved so sacrificially. Come, Holy Spirit, come.

God's Desires

Readings: Hos 6:1-6; Luke 18:9-14

Scripture:
For it is love that I desire, not sacrifice,
   and knowledge of God rather than burnt offerings.
      (Hos 6:6)

Reflection: In 1961, *Report to Greco* was published, an auto-biographical work by Greek author Nikos Kazantzakis. In this work, Kazantzakis tells of his two great desires: the longing for freedom and for sanctity. Whether or not those desires were achieved is a matter of conjecture.

All of us have desires, longings of the mind and heart. God too. The prophet Hosea records that the sacrifice of bulls and calves and the burnt offerings that people felt obliged to make are not what God is looking for. Rather, God desires love and knowledge.

Love! Ironically, this love will be most fully realized in a "sacrifice," the sacrifice of the cross. In giving his life for us, Jesus manifested the essence of love: total self-giving. "This is my body . . . this is my blood, given for you." Indeed, there is no greater love than to give one's life for another. Mothers and fathers, martyrs and prophets, teachers and friends do this. At the heart of doing God's will is the commitment to share with others the love God has given to us. This is the real sacrifice pleasing to God.

Knowledge! Just as the heart seeks to love, so the mind hungers for truth. Ignorance leads to fear and anxiety. Knowledge of God and of our deepest self leads to peace and unity. We are given two major sources for knowledge: reason and faith. By using our intelligence, we come to a partial knowledge of the mysteries of our existence. By appropriating revelation through faith, we trust that what we are told in the Scriptures is truly the word of God. Saint Josephine Bakhita (1869–1947), through reason, faith, and community, came to this marvelous truth: she was created, known, loved, and awaited by God.

In Thornton Wilder's 1942 play *The Skin of Our Teeth*, the character Atrobus has the feeling of lostness. When asked what he has lost, Atrobus simply says, "the desire to begin again," and that, he claims, is the most important thing in life. Every day we are invited to begin again in our loving and knowing.

Meditation: What are the desires of your heart? What roles do love and knowledge play in your life?

Prayer: God of love and truth, send your Spirit into our world. Give us the grace of self-giving and grant us the wisdom to know what really matters. Come, Holy Spirit, come.

Paradox: Light and Darkness

Readings: 1 Sam 16:1b, 6-7, 10-13a; Eph 5:8-14; John 9:1-41 or 9:1, 6-9, 13-17, 34-38

Scripture:
You were once darkness,
 but now you are light in the Lord.
Live as children of light,
 for light produces every kind of goodness
 and righteousness and truth. (Eph 5:8-9)

Reflection: A major theme in Shakespeare's *King Lear* is light and darkness, sight and blindness. Paradoxically, the king failed to see (understand) his daughters, just as another character, Gloucester, blinded by family members, came to "see" the truth about his sons. A great hope of this Lenten season is that we "see better" how good God is, how complex we are, how beautiful and tragic is our world. Though *King Lear* is drama, its themes of sight and blindness permeate the Scriptures as well.

The Lord sent Samuel to Jesse to anoint one of his sons as king. The Lord gave Samuel a special instruction—don't judge by appearance or lofty stature. God's sight looks into the heart, where he sets his seal. Although splendid in appearance, there was something in the youthful David's heart that won God's favor. Samuel anointed David and the Lord's Spirit rushed upon him.

Saint Paul knew darkness and blindness. In his dramatic conversion, Paul could not see for three days. When healed of blindness, this apostle to the Gentiles shared his vision of Jesus as our redeemer and savior. Paul knew that Christ gives us light, love, and life. Paul was raised from darkness and brought into the light of day.

In the gospel Jesus heals a blind man. While the gospel narrative relates the attempt to find the cause of blindness (was it sin?), the message is one of faith. Just as the heart has eyes helping us to be compassionate, so the soul has eyes enabling us to perceive the working of grace. Faith breaks the bonds of darkness; faith in the Lord's resurrection breaks the bonds of death.

In *King Lear* the blind see while the "seeing ones" are sightless. In the gospel the same paradox happens. Jesus said, "I came . . . so that those who do not see might see, / and those who do see might become blind" (John 9:39). May the gift of faith help us walk in the Lord's light.

Meditation: In what sense do we have eyes in our hearts and souls? Why is it so difficult to see truly who we are and what God is doing in our lives?

Prayer: God of light, grant us the gifts of wisdom and understanding. Help us to see the marvelous works of your hand; help us to leave the darkness of sin and follow in your way. Heal us of our blindness.

Trust: A Fundamental Requirement

Readings: Isa 65:17-21; John 4:43-54

Scripture:
Jesus said to him [royal official], "You may go; your son
  will live.
The man believed what Jesus said to him and left.
  (John 4:50)

Reflection: Medical doctors are called upon to deliver messages that sometimes bring great joy, sometimes bring great distress and sorrow. After examining a child, they approach the parents and say, "Your daughter is going to be OK" or "Your son is not going to make it." The emotion that follows is overwhelming.

Jesus, *the* doctor, that is, *the* teacher, conveyed a message of life to the royal official distressed at his son's illness. Then those hope-filled words were spoken: "your son will live." This is the message of resurrection. Illness and death have been conquered by the presence of God in history. The paschal mystery gives us the source of our hope: Jesus, by his life, death, and resurrection, enables us to trust in the promise of eternal life. We can return home to our daily duties and get on with life knowing that even if members of our family die, they share in the hope of immortality.

In *Late Night Thoughts on Listening to Mahler's Ninth Symphony*, Lewis Thomas makes this claim: "Trust is a fundamental requirement for our kind of existence, and without it all our linkages would begin to snap loose." We trust in the pilots who fly from New York to San Francisco without seeing them or knowing their names; we trust teachers and physicians who minister to our children; we trust in the words exchanged in the wedding ceremony. Our existence is grounded in trust. When it is not there, we fall apart.

The royal official *trusted* in Jesus' word. And Jesus speaks to us through Isaiah the prophet that there will be a new heaven and a new earth, that one day our weeping and crying will come to an end, that God will make us his joy and delight.

Meditation: What is your level of trust for God and those with whom you live? Are you trustworthy?

Prayer: Faithful God, you give us your word, your promise of presence. We trust that you are truly with us in our joys and sorrows, in our rising and dying. Help us to believe in your message of life and love; help us to be agents of that love and life in our world today.

April 1: Tuesday of the Fourth Week of Lent

Life's Most Terrifying Burden

Readings: Ezek 47:1-9, 12; John 5:1-16

Scripture:
Now that day was a sabbath.
So the Jews said to the man who was cured,
  "It is the sabbath, and it is not lawful for you to carry
    your mat." (John 5:9b-10)

Reflection: Some mats are heavy, so much so that a single individual might not be able to bear it. And when that person has been sick for thirty-eight years, the likelihood of sufficient strength is in doubt. We are speaking here not about the weight of a physical mat, but the burdens that life imposes on some individuals.

One of the deepest forms of suffering on our long journey is the absence of companionship, especially during serious physical illness, psychological pain, or spiritual dryness. As social beings, we need the support of others at these times. Traveling alone is a dangerous affair, for if we fall, there is no one there to help us up.

Jesus had special concern for those on the margins, for those who were alienated from society, who knew the anxiety of utter loneliness. With empathy, he entered their lives and offered them his compassion and love. He reaffirmed their dignity and helped them to "reconnect" to the larger community. The person Jesus cured of leprosy experienced this, as did the person in today's gospel.

"Sir, I have no one to put me into the pool / when the water is stirred up" (John 5:7a). There are few words more painful than "I have no one!" In *The Denial of Death*, Ernest Becker writes, "The most terrifying burden of the creature is to be isolated, which is what happens in individuation: one separates himself out of the herd." By contrast, the most intense joy comes in communion with others and with God.

Meditation: What has been your experience of "individuation"? Can loneliness have a positive side? Who cares for you; whom do you care for?

Prayer: Compassionate Jesus, help us to understand the depth of human loneliness, both within ourselves and in others. Do not let busyness or trivial entertainment block us from getting in touch with our true selves. May we experience time and time again your indwelling Spirit and realize that we are never alone.

Double Resurrection

Readings: Isa 49:8-15; John 5:17-30

Scripture:
"[T]he hour is coming in which all who are in the tombs
will hear his [the Father's] voice and will come out,
those who have done good deeds
to the resurrection of life,
but those who have done wicked deeds
to the resurrection of condemnation." (John 5:28b-29)

Reflection: Not everyone delights in the message of the mystery of resurrection. In the last judgment scene in Matthew's gospel, where the sheep and goats are separated according to their good or bad deeds, the goats must have wished that there would be no resurrection whatsoever. The judgment rendered against them was not even due to evil deeds but to the fact that they neglected to help those who were in need.

We live in a culture that gives little thought to eschatology, to the last things. Heaven and hell have vanished from the radar screen of the postmodern person. The immediacy of things consume contemporary consciousness, and what happens in the future, if there is a future, is left to letting the cards fall as they may. Jesus proposes another vision. There is an afterlife and the quality of that existence is determined by the doing of good or bad deeds. It is also determined by the mercy of God.

So, do we know of anyone who, because of wickedness, will "rise" to condemnation? We don't know. We do know that some good people, really good people (saints), have been canonized because their lives give evidence of heroic virtue. The church claims that these individuals have experienced the resurrection of life.

During this season of Lent our eyes glance ever so often toward Easter Sunday. We know that we must pass through Calvary and the empty tomb, but our faith assures us that Jesus is the resurrection and life, that the bonds of death have been broken. Hopefully, this faith will lead us to follow in his way of doing good deeds and building the kingdom.

Meditation: What is your understanding of the mystery of the resurrection? Are the concepts of heaven and hell on your radar screen?

Prayer: Jesus, our risen one, send your Spirit of faith and charity into our hearts and into your world. Help us to believe in the afterlife; help us to do good deeds on this long journey of life. May our longing for heaven fill us with zeal for your kingdom.

April 3: Thursday of the Fourth Week of Lent

The Way

Readings: Exod 32:7-14; John 5:31-47

Scripture:
The Lord said to Moses,
  "Go down at once to your people
  whom you brought out of the land of Egypt,
  for they have become depraved.
They have soon turned aside from the way I pointed out
  to them . . ." (Exod 32:7-8a)

Reflection: The call to fidelity is threatened in so many ways. For the Israelite people, struggling on their pilgrimage through the desert, the molten calf became an idol and they turned away from the Lord. In our culture, we find fidelity to God's way—the way of love, compassion, and forgiveness—difficult as well, as we turn to lifestyles characterized by intolerance, incivility, and revenge. Our molten calf is one of radical individualism and doing things "our way." In the air are the lyrics, "I did it my way!"

Jesus came to do the works that his Father gave him to do. Through his teaching, healing, and redemptive ministry, Jesus gives testimony of what "the way" is all about: God's love and mercy flooding the universe. When the love of God is not in our hearts, we act in depraved ways. When the mercy of God is not appropriated and shared, we become a violent people.

In our gospel acclamation we pray, "God so loved the world that he gave his only-begotten Son, / so that everyone who believes in him might have eternal life" (John 3:16). Jesus came to bring life; Jesus came to bring love; Jesus, the true burning and shining lamp, came to bring light into a dark world.

In his work *The Prophetic Imagination*, the Scripture scholar Walter Brueggemann claims that a prophet helps both to bring "hope to public expression" and "to return the community to its single referent, the sovereign faithfulness of God." God's way is one of fidelity. Made to the image and likeness of God, we too are called to be faithful to a God who loves and awaits us. Moses was faithful to God's call; Jesus was faithful in doing the Father's will. Our call is essentially the same.

Meditation: What is your understanding of fidelity? What temptations do you encounter both from our culture and within your heart?

Prayer: Faithful and true God, we turn aside so easily from your way, walking in darkness and chasing idols. Grant us the grace to be faithful to your way. Help us to name our idols and to seek forgiveness. May we experience once again your mercy and love.

Being Good/Doing Good

Readings: Wis 2:1a, 12-22; John 7:1-2, 10, 25-30

Scripture:
"To us he [the just one] is the censure of our thoughts;
    merely to see him is a hardship for us,
Because his life is not like that of others,
    and different are his ways. (Wis 2:14-15)

Reflection: Why are good people irritating? One would think that virtuous individuals would be a blessing to be around, for are they not kind, considerate, caring folks? Yet, their very presence triggers something in us that may make us feel judged or wanting in moral integrity. And this is not due to their being obnoxious, but simply because our personal darkness does not like the light.

Jesus irritated the authorities in Jerusalem, so much so that they plotted to kill him. When Pope John Paul II visited Austria in June of 1988, it was discovered that an attempt on his life was being planned. Evil abhors goodness; darkness fears the light; a good person is, simply by being present, a reproach to bad people.

Classical spiritual writers tell us that concupiscence, "the rebellion of the sensual appetites" (Aelred Squire), does two things: weakens our willpower and blinds us from seeing the truth of things. And, of course, if the mind cannot see and the will is weakened, our behavior will not be just, courageous, or prudent. Our moral life will be chaotic.

History is filled with just people who were being killed. Abraham Lincoln was detested by those who favored slavery. Gandhi was assassinated as he worked to liberate his people from colonial oppression. John the Baptist was beheaded by the incensed Herod and his resentful wife. Not only would the killers and assassins find it a hardship to look at the presence of goodness, but their wickedness would attempt to destroy those very moral qualities that they themselves so utterly lacked.

Individuals whose moral conduct is upright and just are bound to find opposition and even oppression because they are different and not like the people of a given dominant culture. Jesus and the prophets, just and upright people, were willing to pay the price of rejection in being true to their mission.

Meditation: What does evil and wickedness do to our minds and hearts? How do you feel in the presence of a truly good, just person? Do any negative emotions arise?

Prayer: God of justice and love, instill in us the integrity and courage we need to live a truly moral and spiritual life. We are weak; evil is around and within us. Without your grace we are bound to fail. Help us to rejoice in goodness; help us to combat evil.

Searcher of Mind and Heart

Readings: Jer 11:18-20; John 7:40-53

Scripture:
But, you, O Lord of hosts, O just Judge,
    searcher of mind and heart,
Let me witness the vengeance you take on them,
    for to you I have entrusted my cause! (Jer 11:20)

Reflection: Psalm 139 is eloquent in its expression of the mystery of God: "Lord, you have probed [searched] me, you know me: / you know when I sit and stand; / you understand my thoughts from afar" (139:1-2, NABRE). The concept of God as a searcher is intriguing. Not only is God aware of our deeds—our sitting down and standing, our eating and drinking, our working and playing—but God also looks into the depth of our minds and hearts. It is there, in our thoughts and affections, conscious and unconscious, that God casts his loving, compassionate glance.

Jesus, *the* prophet, was a searcher. He sought out Peter and Andrew, James and John, Matthew and Zacchaeus, the Samaritan woman at the well, you and me. He also sought out Nicodemus, who came to Jesus in the night, a good man who had a sense of justice. Jesus, like the "hound of heaven" in Francis Thompson's poem, pursues us down the nights and down the days, seeking to bring us his Father's truth, peace, and joy.

Just as God searches our minds and hearts, we too search. We are looking for something or someone. Our longings go beyond food and drink, sexuality and fame, power and possessions. We have infinite longings, an incredible desire for fullness of being. Nothing finite satisfies us, not even the best friendship or greatest success. We are made for God and our restlessness remains until we welcome God into our lives as the divine guest.

The poet Robert Frost's search for truth and meaning came primarily from his experience of nature, not from educational or ecclesial institutions. Some find God in nature; some find God in an academic setting; some find God in sacraments and Scripture. But let us not be fooled. It is God who seeks us much more than we who seek God.

Meditation: Are you a searcher? What are you looking for? Is the image of God as a searcher part of your faith understanding?

Prayer: O God, you who search us out day by day, grant us the grace to stand still and encounter you. May we offer you our hospitality; may we welcome you into our minds and hearts. And as you seek us out, may we search for you in our everyday experience for you are always near.

The Spirit of Christ

Readings: Ezek 37:12-14; Rom 8:8-11; John 11:1-45 or 11:3-7, 17, 20-27, 33b-45

Scripture:
But you are not in the flesh;
on the contrary, you are in the spirit,
if only the Spirit of God dwells in you.
Whoever does not have the Spirit of Christ does not
belong to him. (Rom 8:9)

Reflection: In today's gospel Jesus' tears were certainly for his friend Lazarus but also for Martha and Mary, Lazarus's sisters. And, in confronting the universal reality of death, those tears may have been for all of us who have lost loved ones and who one day must die.

Beneath those tears was the spirit of compassion. Jesus felt deeply the pain and suffering of others. That compassion was manifest as Jesus raised up the son of the widow of Naim, as Jesus forgave the adulterous woman and let the accusers—themselves not innocent—walk away, as Jesus gave Jairus back his daughter. Jesus, the compassionate one; Jesus, the suffering servant.

Saint Paul reminds the Romans that the Spirit of Christ dwells within them. Indeed, if we do not have compassion and love for others, we do not belong to Christ; we cannot claim discipleship. Like Jesus, we are to identify with those who suffer, reach out to those in need, visit the sick and imprisoned. The Spirit of Christ is active and demanding. Compassion should be a way of life for the Christian community.

But then we read about Shylock in Shakespeare's *The Merchant of Venice*. Shylock, the Jew, is persecuted by Christians and a famous passage questions whether Christians of Venice had the Spirit of Christ: "I am a Jew. Hath not a Jew eyes? Hath not a Jew hands, organs, dimensions, senses, passions? Fed with the same food, hurt with the same weapons, subject to the same diseases, heal'd by the same means, warm'd and cool'd by the same winter and summer, as a Christian is? . . . If you wrong us, shall we not revenge? If we are like you in the rest, we will resemble you in that."

Just as Paul comments on the Spirit of Christ dwelling in us, Ezekiel in the first reading tells of God's promise to put the divine spirit in us and settle with us in our true country. Is not that spirit one of compassion? Is not our true country a compassionate one? Let us hope and pray that it is.

Meditation: What is your understanding of compassion? Who are the compassionate people who have been part of your history?

Prayer: Compassionate and loving Lord, send your Spirit into our lives. May we feel what you feel; may your concerns be ours. May we build your kingdom of compassion today.

Two Human Stories

Readings: Dan 13:1-9, 15-17, 19-30, 33-62 or 13:41c-62;
John 8:1-11

Scripture:
But when they [the scribes and Pharisees] continued
  asking him,
  he straightened up and said to them,
    "Let the one among you who is without sin
    be the first to throw a stone at her." (John 8:7)

Reflection: Hypocrisy is not foreign to any of us. It was not
foreign to the scribes and Pharisees; it was not foreign to the
two old men who attempted to seduce Susanna; it is not
foreign whenever we stand in judgment of others' sins while
we ourselves stand in need of forgiveness. By some strange
quirk, we have the incredible ability to see the speck in our
neighbor's eye while being blind to the beam in our own.

Jesus and Daniel are our wisdom figures. They are
"judges" who take us into the truth of things. Jesus invites
the sinless one to throw the first stone; Daniel cleverly ferrets
out the perjury of the two old men. What makes these biblical
stories so powerful and memorable is their capacity to hold
up a mirror to our own lives. All of us have sinned; all of us
stand in need of God's mercy. All of us must stop throwing
stones.

And the two women: Susanna and the anonymous woman caught in adultery! And the men: the scribes and Pharisees and the two elders! And the two agents of God: Jesus and Daniel! As the stories unfold, we begin to identify with one group or the others. Sometimes we are the victims of sin, sometimes the sinner, sometimes the instrument of justice and mercy.

In her novel *O Pioneers!* Willa Cather writes, "There are only two or three human stories, and they go on repeating themselves as fiercely as if they had never happened before; like the larks in this country, that have been singing the same five notes over for thousands of years." Two of those stories are stories of sin and grace. And Jesus stands in the middle of them.

Meditation: Why is throwing stones so dangerous? What are the five notes in your story?

Prayer: God of love and mercy, help us to live your story of grace. May we never throw stones at others; may we be always agents of justice and truth; may we have compassionate hearts. Come, Lord Jesus, come.

Generations and Cultures

Readings: Num 21:4-9; John 8:21-30

Scripture:
But with their patience worn out by the journey,
   the people complained against God and Moses,
   "Why have you brought us up from Egypt to die in this
      desert . . . ?" (Num 21:4b-5a)

Reflection: Sociologists have the practice of labeling things, such things as generations and cultures. Thus, we are given the Lost Generation (1883–1900), the Silent Generation (1925–42), the Baby Boomers (1946–64), the Millennial Generation (1982–2000), among others. Individuals and nations during these time periods exhibit particular qualities that distinguish them from one another.

And what about cultures? Cultures have to do with "the way things are done around here!" That "doing of things" might be in terms of dance, foods, politics, education, or any other aspect of life. Again sociologists attempt to find labels that describe, as much as possible, dominant trends.

God and Moses were not sociologists, as far as I know. But if they had to name the culture that came out of Egypt after the great liberation, they might have called it "A Culture of Complaint"! Nothing was right: the food was wretched; the desert gave off the odor of death; water supply was almost nonexistent. The complaints arose out of their patience being worn out because of this tedious, painful journey.

Jesus, whatever sociological instincts he had, also had to deal with complaints day in and day out. The disciples were looking for places of honor; the authorities were out to kill him; even Martha complained that her brother would not have died *if* Jesus had been there. Complaining, whining, dissatisfaction, nothing is ever good enough—markings of a culture of complaint. We can almost hear a divine shout: "Grow up!"

Meditation: What do you do when your patience is worn out? When is complaining healthy and when is it neurotic? What is it that will satisfy our human longings?

Prayer: God of Moses and Abraham and Isaac, give us the grace of patience. May we embrace the tough times as much as the good times. Help us to endure our daily cross and give us the wisdom to complain when and if it is in accordance with your will. Preserve us from becoming curmudgeons.

The Fourth Man

Readings: Dan 3:14-20, 91-92, 95; John 8:31-42

Scripture:
Nebuchadnezzar rose in haste and asked his nobles,
  "Did we not cast three men bound into the fire? . . .
But . . . I see four men unfettered and unhurt,
  walking in the fire, and the fourth looks like a son of
    God." (Dan 3:91-92)

Reflection: Spiritual writers remind us time and time again that the spiritual life is about participating in the holy presence of God. God is everywhere and if we behold the divine presence and respond to it, we are leading a spiritual life. By contrast, nonattention to God's abiding love and light means that we have chosen a nonspiritual way of existence.

The prophet Daniel narrates the powerful story of the faith life of Shadrach, Meshach, and Abednego. Even in the midst of trial and suffering, they blessed their God who was with them. And old king Nebuchadnezzar was given a vision of God's presence as a fourth figure in the fiery furnace. In the end, even the king had a change of heart and blessed the God of Shadrach, Meshach, and Abednego.

Jesus lived in the presence of his Father: "I tell you what I have seen in the Father's presence; / then do what you have heard from the Father" (John 8:38). The work given to

Jesus was that of redemption, the restoration of unity. He came to set all of us free from the slavery of sin. This mystery of reconciliation has been handed on to us.

The problem that faced Nebuchadnezzar and the descendants of Abraham and all of us is the "golden statue." Whether that idol is one of wealth or self-will or power, every generation has to deal with the sin of idolatry. Whatever the sin is, it separates us from the living and true God revealed in Jesus. Whether we admit it or not, sin enslaves and pulls us down just as gravity does. Our hope lies in that "fourth man," in the presence of God's Spirit ever abiding in our midst. Whatever the dark night of the soul or the fiery furnace we find ourselves in, God is at our side. Even the blind Nebuchadnezzar was given the vision to see the divine presence.

Meditation: In what ways do you participate in the holy presence of God? Do you have to struggle with the experience of nonattention?

Prayer: God of Shadrach, Meshach, and Abednego, be with us on this perilous journey. Without your Spirit, we are vulnerable to the sin of idolatry. Help us to be faithful, help us to be courageous in doing your will.

Self-Identity

Readings: Gen 17:3-9; John 8:51-59

Scripture:
So the Jews said to him [Jesus], . . .
"Are you greater than our father Abraham, who died?
Or the prophets, who died?
Who do you make yourself out to be?" (John 8:53)

Reflection: The question of self-identity is of major importance to all of us. Perhaps the question addressed to Jesus needs reformulation. Not "Who do you make yourself out to be?" but, rather, "What is the very essence of your identity?" Jesus' "I AM" is mysterious and filled with deep meaning.

So who are we in the light of the Scripture? According to Isaiah, we are the beloved of God and called by name (Isa 43:1-4). Saint Paul reminds us that we are stewards of the mysteries of God (1 Cor 4:1). Jesus himself says we are no longer servants but friends. Beloved! Stewards! Friends! Because of God's providence, we too will not taste death, the kind of death that so many individuals consider simple annihilation.

Abraham and the prophets were messengers of God. They had a vision of life that transcended time and space. Called into a deep love relationship (covenant) with God, they lived their lives with God, with God being their reference point.

Their vocation was to draw people into the radius of God's benevolent grace.

Our Lenten challenge is to discern what God has made us to be. We are not in the enterprise of constructing our own identity. Rather, it is the adventure of being grasped by God, a God who "hounds" us down the nights and down the days. Wise are those who stop running. Wise are those who, like Abraham and the prophets, yield to God's covenantal love.

Meditation: What type of identity have you tried to construct for yourself? What type of covenant have you and God made?

Prayer: God of Abraham and the prophets, draw near to us and empower us to experience the mystery of your love. Too long have we tried to find our identity as autonomous creatures. Give us the vision to see your image within us; give us the courage to live that image every day.

The Place

Readings: Jer 20:10-13; John 10:31-42

Scripture:
He went back across the Jordan
   to the place where John first baptized, and there he
      remained. (John 10:40)

Reflection: It was at the Jordan that Jesus underwent his baptism. Though John the Baptist protested when Jesus approached the river, he yielded, and Jesus, the Lamb of God, began his public ministry. Now, in today's gospel, as Jesus faced the threat of death by stoning, he returned to *the place*, the place where the words "You are my beloved Son" were spoken. By returning to the Jordan, Jesus again felt the reassurance and grace to complete his ministry to the end.

And what about Jeremiah? He too found opposition and denouncement, persecution and vengeance. Just as Jesus returned to the site of confirmation, Jeremiah turned within to prayer, praying to God who rescues the lives of the poor. It was from that inner place that Jeremiah knew God to be his mighty champion.

Jesus and Jeremiah were in distress. Like them, we might put to heart our responsorial refrain: "In my distress I called upon the Lord, and he heard my voice" (Ps 18:7a). We might establish a *place* (a den, a lake, a woods, a rocking chair) where we withdraw from our busy lives and seek some solitude and silence. There, in that place, we wait upon the Lord in our emptiness. Through the gift of faith, we are convinced that God is there, a mighty champion, a beloved friend, a healing redeemer.

Meditation: Do you have a "sacred" place where you experience God in a unique way? Do you invite others to that sacred ground?

Prayer: Loving God, mighty champion, come to us in our distress. The burdens of life are many; the troubles abundant. May the consolation you give us help us to assist our sisters and brothers who bear heavy burdens. May they find a caring place in our hearts.

Present and Manifest

Readings: Ezek 37:21-28; John 11:45-56

Scripture:
My dwelling shall be with them;
   I will be their God, and they shall be my people.
      (Ezek 37:27)

Reflection: The Anglican theologian John Macquarrie speaks repeatedly of God being present and manifest, emphasizing the nearness of God as well as the revelation of the Christian deity. In Jesus, God is present and manifest, here and now. What we read about in Ezekiel, we find realized in the gospel.

Strange to say (or not so strange), the divine presence was a threat to those in authority. Further, Jesus' claim to intimacy with the Father was viewed as blasphemy, worthy of the death penalty. Regardless, Jesus continued his mission of reconciling the world to the Father.

The gospel acclamation articulates the imperatives that make possible our experiencing of God's abiding presence and manifestation: "Cast away from you all the crimes you have committed, says the Lord, and make for yourselves a new heart and a new spirit" (Ezek 18:31). Where crimes and sins abound, the presence of God is obscured. With a new heart and a new spirit, we will recognize how God is manifest in the cry of the poor, in simple acts of kindness, in the richness of creation and our sacramental life. This acclamation gives us the *sine qua non* for spiritual vision and a committed response.

In the musical *My Fair Lady*, we hear, "Don't talk of love, show me!" Talk is one thing, doing is another. Our God, a God of love, not only speaks his word but also comes to us to make present and manifest the mystery of self-giving.

Meditation: When do you sense God's presence? How are God's love and mercy manifest to you? How do you manifest that love and mercy to others?

Prayer: Lord Jesus, give us a new heart and a new spirit. Then, and only then, will we be your people and you be our God. Too often we are blind to your blazing presence; too often we are oblivious to your ubiquitous manifestations.

Usque ad Mortem (Even unto Death)

Readings: Matt 21:1-11; Isa 50:4-7; Phil 2:6-11; Matt 26:14–27:66 or 27:11-54

Scripture:
[Jesus was] human in appearance,
he humbled himself,
becoming obedient to the point of death,
even death on a cross. (Phil 2:7-8)

Reflection: The great hymn given to us in St. Paul's letter to the Philippians recapitulates the great Christian narrative. We are told how, in the mystery of the incarnation, Jesus emptied himself, how through his obedience to the Father's will he offered himself in the supreme sacrifice of the cross, how the Father exalted and raised Jesus up as our Lord. Paul knew well that here, in the paschal mystery, is the essence of our faith.

Songs do carry our theology. Our hymns remind us of who we are and who God is. How dangerous it is to forget the melodies that chart our journey back to the mystery of God. If our faith is truly deep, despite the doubts that assail us, then we experience what one tradition hums: "How can we keep from singing?"

But all of this is grounded in the passion of our Lord, in Jesus' obedience, even unto death. It is in fear and trembling that we witness the sufferings of Christ: Judas's betrayal, Peter's denial, the physical torture and crucifixion, the psychological pain, the sense of spiritual abandonment. While our eyes are set on Easter Sunday, we cannot experience the joy of the resurrection without the painful path of Good Friday.

George Eliot, in her novel *Adam Bede*, offers this psychological insight: "Energetic natures, strong for all strenuous deeds, will often rush away from a hopeless sufferer, as if they were hard-hearted. It is the over-mastering sense of pain that drives them." The disciples were people of "energetic natures" and graced sensitivity. Yet, that "over-mastering sense of pain" led them to disassociate themselves from the great "sufferer," the Lord Jesus. They were not hard-hearted. They were afraid, as we all are, of pain and of having to watch others suffer.

Meditation: What is your reaction to suffering and death? What meaning does the mystery of the cross play in your spiritual life?

Prayer: Lord Jesus, you taught us how to live and how to die. Grant us the grace of obedience and courage. May we never abandon you whatever the situation. May we share in your passion so that we may also share in your resurrection.

April 14: Monday of Holy Week

Our Light and Our Salvation

Readings: Isa 42:1-7; John 12:1-11

Scripture:
The Lord is my light and my salvation;
   whom should I fear?
The Lord is my life's refuge;
   of whom should I be afraid? (Ps 27:1-2)

Reflection: The prophet Isaiah sings about God's chosen one who is a light to the nations, the one who will establish peace and justice on the earth. This servant is filled with compassion, protecting the bruised reed and the smoldering wick. Whatever is vulnerable gets his attention. The mission of the servant is light and salvation.

Jesus is that servant, bringing life to Lazarus and offering salvation to Judas. But the Iscariot is a thief and a betrayer, a person who lives in darkness and violence. Though light and love and salvation were offered to him, the mystery of evil held Judas bound. Even though Jesus offered him friendship, Judas refused the gift.

Martha and Mary were offered the same gift, the grace of friendship. Martha responded by serving a meal and Mary by preparing Jesus for burial. They lived in Jesus' light and love. They had nothing to fear.

The last stanza of the responsorial psalm reads "I believe that I shall see the bounty of the LORD / in the land of the living. / Wait for the LORD with courage; / be stouthearted, and wait for the LORD" (Ps 27:13-14). During this Holy Week we all need courage to travel to Calvary and witness again both the mystery of sin and the mystery of God's extravagant love. Glancing at the cross we see our light and our salvation, a bruised reed crushed for us, a smoldering wick extinguished momentarily but then bursting into flame once again.

Meditation: How do you deal with the paradox of light and darkness in our world, in your own heart? How have you experienced God as your light and your salvation?

Prayer: Compassionate and loving God, you are the light that shines in our darkness, our salvation that gives us hope. Give us courage and compassion to be true disciples; give us faith and love to follow your son Jesus.

Polished Arrows in God's Quiver

Readings: Isa 49:1-6; John 13:21-33, 36-38

Scripture:
He [the Lord] made me a polished arrow,
  in his quiver he hid me.
You are my servant, he said to me,
  Israel, through whom I show my glory. (Isa 49:2a-3)

Reflection: God has many polished arrows in his quiver. Isaiah the prophet was one of them. He was faithful in delivering God's message, the message of a suffering servant who would save the world. What anxiety Isaiah must have felt as he gazed upon the world, filled with so much brutality and violence, while being given a vision of God's glory and life. Prophets suffer greatly in their awareness of the gap between God's plan and the misuse of human freedom.

Peter was a polished arrow, hidden in God's vast quiver. He was committed to Jesus and specially chosen for a leadership role. But this arrow, like all of us, was tarnished. He had to deal with his personal fears and cowardice. Though he would deny Jesus, before the morning cock crowed twice, he would repent and go on to give his life for the kingdom.

And, yes, Judas too was a polished arrow. He was chosen by Jesus as one of the Twelve. He was given responsibilities and he was trusted. But then he sinned. He stole; he lied; he betrayed his master. "Satan entered him. . . . And it was night" (John 13:27a, 30b). A glorious, shining arrow was darkened and broken. God's quiver suffered a severe loss.

Through baptism and confirmation, we are called and chosen to follow in the Lord's way. Our true country is in God's quiver, on the alert to do God's bidding.

Meditation: Who are the people in your life who have made their home in God's quiver? How do you keep your arrow polished?

Prayer: Lord Jesus, help us to be faithful and loyal to your mission. May we, your polished arrows, give glory to the Father by doing our duty and enduring our cross. Give us your courage and wisdom.

"Morning after Morning"

Readings: Isa 50:4-9a; Matt 26:14-25

Scripture:
Morning after morning
   he opens my ear that I may hear;
And I have not rebelled,
   have not turned back. (Isa 50:4b-5)

Reflection: The poet e. e. cummings ends one of his poems, after giving thanks to God for an "amazing day," by proclaiming that now his ears are awake and his eyes are open. What a grace, to truly hear and to truly see. Much of our life is spent in deafness and blindness, in not seeing or hearing. No wonder we miss so many "amazing days," so much grace.

Judas Iscariot did not see well. He was blind to Jesus' great love for him. Judas listened, not to the stirrings of the Holy Spirit, but to the voice of greed and betrayal. He failed in gratitude, not appreciating how blessed he was and what dignity he possessed. And in saying, "Surely it is not I, Rabbi?" Judas revealed his lack of honesty and integrity.

Jesus, the suffering servant, had not only open ears ("Morning after morning") but also an obedient heart. We pray in the gospel acclamation, "Hail to you, our King, obedient to the Father; / you were led to your crucifixion like a gentle lamb to the slaughter." No rebellion here, no turning away from the painful work of salvation. In emptying himself and accepting death, Jesus witnessed to the fact that it was his Father's will that governed his life.

And our ears and eyes? How open are they and how full are we of gratitude and fidelity? Every day is amazing. Every morning we must beg God to open our ears and our eyes to the mystery of divine love and mercy.

Meditation: How well do you see and hear? How does God speak to you? How does God show you his glory?

Prayer: Gracious Father, we find it so difficult to be attentive to your voice and aware of your presence. Open our eyes and ears, our minds and hearts—morning after morning. May we be obedient and faithful to your call.

Holy Thursday: Celebration and Commitment

Readings: Exod 12:1-8, 11-14; 1 Cor 11:23-26; John 13:1-15

Scripture:
"This day shall be a memorial feast for you,
   which all your generations shall celebrate
   with pilgrimage to the Lord, as a perpetual institution."
   (Exod 12:14)

Reflection: There are days and then there are days. The Jewish people celebrated the great event of liberation from Egypt, for them the land of slavery. Christians, freed from sin and death through the paschal mystery, celebrate year after year a memorial of the Last Supper. As St. Paul recounts, the self-giving of Jesus in his Body and Blood has been handed on to us as a perpetual institution.

We are all on pilgrimage. We are all travelers who need physical and spiritual nourishment, the support of the community, and advice on how to live. At the Last Supper a meal was shared, words were spoken, and an example was given. Eucharist was not just the self-giving of Jesus but also a call to serve, be that as a parent, a doctor or nurse, or someone who washes the feet of those in need.

Two effects of a graced celebration of the Lord's Supper are a deepening of friendship with Christ and an ever-increasing expansion of service to others. Jesus loved those who were at table with him and understood the burdens that each one carried. Jesus challenged those who were with him at table to accept the call to feed the hungry, clothe the naked, tend to those who need a healing touch. Our Holy Thursday celebration has the power to transform our lives.

At many parishes, as Sunday Mass is concluded, worshipers are told that they are now entering the mission field. Holy Thursday is both a celebration and a commitment.

Meditation: How has your understanding of the Eucharist grown over the years? Is your experience of Holy Thursday both a celebration and a commitment?

Prayer: Jesus, we gather at the table to hear your word and to receive the gift of you. Open our minds and hearts to this incredible mystery. Strengthen us to live a life of dedicated service. Come, Lord Jesus, come.

Tremble, Tremble, Tremble

Readings: Isa 52:13–53:12; Heb 4:14-16; 5:7-9; John 18:1–19:42

Scripture:
When Jesus saw his mother and the disciple there whom
    he loved
  he said to his mother, "Woman, behold, your son."
Then he said to the disciple,
  "Behold, your mother." (John 19:26-27a)

Reflection: "Were you there . . . ?" If we stand beneath the cross on Calvary, our souls will "tremble, tremble, tremble!" How could they not as we witness the agony of our crucified Lord. So overwhelming are the mysteries of suffering and death that we become inarticulate, and we do little but shudder.

"Were you there . . . ?" As they took down the body of Jesus and placed him in the arms of Mary, surely the bystanders "trembled, trembled, trembled!" What agony pierced Mary's heart as she witnessed the cruelty inflicted upon her son, her only son. The bonding between Mary and Jesus was so deep that she felt every blow of the hammer, every word of ridicule, every piercing thorn. What a double crucifixion we have here, both of body and soul.

There is a danger here—the loss of the ability to tremble. Exposed to so much violence in our world and through the mass media, we can become immune to the sufferings of others, even the suffering of Calvary. The challenge is to retain a deep sense of compassion without being overwhelmed by the volume of pain.

So Mary, Jesus' mother, inquires, "Were you there . . . ?" Are you there on this Good Friday to experience once again the extravagance of God's love in Jesus' sacrifice, as well as the horror of sin? A tough question demanding an honest answer.

Meditation: How do you retain a sense of compassion without developing compassion fatigue? When do you shudder and tremble?

Prayer: Crucified Lord, we are overwhelmed by your sacrifice. Help us to understand the extent of our mercy and love. Help us to understand the destructiveness of sin and violence. Mary, pray for us.

Standby: Lights, Camera, Action!

Readings: Gen 1:1–2:2 or 1:1, 26-31a; Gen 22:1-18 or 22:1-2, 9a, 10-13, 15-18; Exod 14:15–15:1; Isa 54:5-14; Isa 55:1-11; Bar 3:9-15, 32–4:4; Ezek 36:16-17a, 18-28; Rom 6:3-11; Matt 28:1-10

Scripture:
"Do not be afraid!
I know that you are seeking Jesus the crucified.
He is not here, for he has been raised just as he said."
(Matt 28:5-6)

Reflection: "Lights! Camera! Action!" The cry on the movie set cannot compare to the Easter Vigil's "Alleluia! Alleluia! Alleluia!" On the most sacred of nights, we praise God as we light our Easter candle, bless the water for baptism, and celebrate again on Holy Thursday. No camera can capture the eucharistic action filled with the light of God's glory.

We praise God for calling our catechumens and candidates into full communion in the church. Over these many weeks of preparation they have been studying God's word and praying for enlightenment. Now they come to receive the risen Lord into their hearts. Then they are sent forth to go and tell the world the good news of our salvation. "Alleluia!"

We praise God for the renewal of our own baptism. We once again renounce sin, testify to our belief in our triune

God, and reaffirm our faith in the communion of saints, the forgiveness of sins, and the resurrection of the body. Because of Jesus, we are promised life everlasting. "Alleluia!"

We praise God for calling us to be an Easter people, for calling us from darkness to light, from death to life. Our vocation is one of being agents of God's light and life, sharing with all we meet the graces given. This agency will have its costs, a sharing in the painful ministry of Jesus, his sacrificial self-offering. But in the giving of self, we experience the Lord's Easter joy and peace. "Alleluia!"

Meditation: What does it mean to be an Easter people? In what sense does the Easter mystery continue to embrace the Calvary passion?

Prayer: Risen Lord, we praise and glorify you. You have set us free from our sins and called us to be your disciples. For that liberation we are grateful; for your call, we give you thanks. Send your Spirit to make us your Easter people.

Resurrection: A Way Out

Readings: Acts 10:34a, 37-43; Col 3:1-4; John 20:1-9

Scripture:
"They put him [Jesus] to death by hanging him on a tree. This man God raised on the third day and granted that he be visible . . ." (Acts 10:39b-40)

Reflection: Saint Paul puts all the cards on the table: If there is no resurrection, our faith is in vain. If death annihilates the individual and the community, we live in a meaningless universe. All the cards are on the table and each of us must make a choice.

In his Gifford Lectures on the varieties of religious experience, William James draws a haunting image. Humankind is on a frozen lake surrounded by high cliffs and the ice is slowly melting. The cliffs are too steep to climb and everyone is doomed. There is "no exit," as the existentialists say.

Christian faith says there is a way out. Jesus, the Son of God, came to live among us and inform us that he is the gateway to eternal life. In fact, he has gone ahead of us to prepare a place for us. We are bound, not for the bottom of the lake, but for the light of glory.

This is Good News; this is Easter joy. Life trumps death. The tomb is empty. Jesus has risen.

Back to James's frozen lake. Reason alone offers little hope. The ice is melting, the cliffs are imposing, no exit is in sight. But faith offers an alternative vision and a blessed hope. Yes, we will die as surely as our ancestors who have come and gone. But faith carries a promise—that where Jesus has gone, we are to follow. We too will pass through the blinding mystery of death—that dark, dark mystery—and come through it into a whole new life. Out of the shadows and into the light, as C. S. Lewis and John Henry Newman tell us. Reason is stopped short at the gate of mystery.

Our Easter joy is not arrogant, but somewhat muted. Many of our brothers and sisters live without faith, without hope. Paul's assertion is not embraced. Yet, they too will glimpse something of Easter joy if we approach them with charity and understanding.

Meditation: How do reason and faith shape your vision of life? Does the frozen lake image speak to you of the human condition?

Prayer: Risen Lord, grant us the gift of faith to believe truly in the mystery of the resurrection. Our vision is so limited; our reason so shallow. Send the gift of your Spirit to enlighten our minds and enkindle our hearts. Fill us with Easter joy and peace, we pray.

References

Introduction
C. S. Lewis, *The Great Divorce* (New York: HarperCollins, 2001), 74.

March 6: Thursday after Ash Wednesday
Alan Paton, *Towards the Mountain* (New York: Scribner's Sons, 1980), 59.

March 7: Friday after Ash Wednesday
William Shakespeare, *Hamlet*, III, iii, 70–71.

———, *King Lear*, III, vi, 74.

March 9: First Sunday of Lent
Karl Rahner, SJ, *The Need and the Blessing of Prayer*, trans. Bruce W. Gillette (Collegeville, MN: Liturgical Press, 1997), 93.

March 10: Monday of the First Week of Lent
William Shakespeare, *Hamlet*, IV, vii, 117–18.

———, *Julius Caesar*, IV, iii, 218–24.

March 12: Wednesday of the First Week of Lent
Fyodor Dostoyevskyhttp, *The Brothers Karamazov* (New York: Macmillan, 1922), 628.

March 13: Thursday of the First Week of Lent
Raissa Maritain, *Raissa's Journal* (Albany, NY: Magi Books, 1974), 225.

March 14: Friday of the First Week of Lent
Romano Guardini, *The Lord* (Chicago: Henry Regnery, 1954), 37.

March 15: Saturday of the First Week of Lent
Erich Fromm, *The Art of Loving* (New York: Continuum, 2000), 25.

George Herbert, "Matins," in *The Temple* (1633).

March 16: Second Sunday of Lent
Ralph Waldo Emerson, "Experience," in *Essays: Second Series* (1844).

March 17: Monday of the Second Week of Lent
The Confessions of St. Augustine, trans. F. J. Sheed (New York: Sheed & Ward, 1943), 79.

C. S. Lewis, *A Grief Observed* (New York: HarperCollins, 1961), 66.

March 18: Tuesday of the Second Week of Lent
Peter Hebblethwaite, *Paul VI: The First Modern Pope* (New York: Paulist Press, 1993), 265.

Nathaniel Hawthorne, *The Scarlet Letter* (Boston: Osgood, 1871), 302.

March 27: Thursday of the Third Week of Lent
C. S. Lewis, *The Screwtape Letters* (New York: HarperCollins, 2009), 99.

March 31: Monday of the Fourth Week of Lent
Lewis Thomas, *Late Night Thoughts on Listening to Mahler's Ninth Symphony* (New York: Bantam Books, 1980), 129.

April 1: Tuesday of the Fourth Week of Lent
Ernest Becker, *The Denial of Death* (New York: Free Press, 1973), 171.

April 3: Thursday of the Fourth Week of Lent
Walter Brueggemann, *The Prophetic Imagination* (New York: Fortress Press, 1978), 68.

April 6: Fifth Sunday of Lent
William Shakespeare, *The Merchant of Venice*, III, i, 51–64.

April 7: *Monday of the Fifth Week of Lent*
Willa Cather, *O Pioneers!* (Boston: Houghton Mifflin, 1913), 119.

April 13: *Palm Sunday of the Lord's Passion*
George Eliot, *Adam Bede* (Chicago: Belford, Clarke, 1888), 384.